T0272445

HOPURANGI—SONGCATCHER

AUCKLAND
UNIVERSITY
PRESS

HOPURANGI—SONGCATCHER

POEMS FROM THE MARAMATAKA

Robert Sullivan

First published 2024
Auckland University Press
Waipapa Taumata Rau
University of Auckland
Private Bag 92019
Auckland 1142
New Zealand
www.aucklanduniversitypress.co.nz

© Robert Sullivan, 2024

ISBN 978 1 77671 122 2

Published with the assistance
of Creative New Zealand

ARTS COUNCIL OF NEW ZEALAND TOI AOTEAROA

A catalogue record for this book is available from
the National Library of New Zealand.

This book is copyright. Apart from fair dealing for the
purpose of private study, research, criticism or review,
as permitted under the Copyright Act, no part may
be reproduced by any process without prior
permission of the publisher. The moral rights
of the author have been asserted.

Design and cover art by Breeze Durham
This book was printed on FSC® certified paper
Printed in Singapore by Markono Print Media Pte Ltd

I dedicate this book to my father, Bob Conlon,
and his brothers and sisters who have passed away.
They're with Nana Sarah and Grandad Paddy now.

Contents

Introduction

I wrote these poems while learning about the Maramataka or Māori lunar calendar, and also while rejoining Facebook after six years. I decided to post a poem a day, and began to notice the different energies as described in the Maramataka resources available online and in print including Wiremu Tāwhai's *Living by the Moon*, Professor Rangi Mātāmua's *Living by the Stars* and Rereata Mākiha's videos online pertaining to the knowledge of our karani from the Ngāti Hau / Ngāti Kaharau hapū of Ngāpuhi. As always, I write about my mother's beloved Ngāti Manu village of Kāretu which continues to give our family strength.

This book covers a period of personal change and growth, reconnecting with my late father's iwi. As well as our Ngāti Manu marae in Te Tai Tokerau, I belong to the Puketeraki Marae of my father's people of Kāti Huirapa, Te Ruahikihiki, Kāti Māmoe, Waitaha, Hāwea, Rapuwai and Kāi Tahu Whānui in Te Tai o Āraiteuru in East Otago.

It is set during three months, Te Ono o Whitiānaunau, Te Whitu o Hakihea, overlapping into Te Waru o Rehua. These poems were written on each day indicated of the Maramataka.

There are many spelling variations for the Maramataka phases. I've chosen to follow the spelling set out in Wiremu Tāwhai's *Living by the Moon*.

Ngā mihi whakawhetai nui ki a koutou katoa e whai i te arohanui o ō tātou mātua tūpuna.

Before the Maramataka

Pāua Canticle

I muscled through tides

between rocks and air, sand turning

like a child's water wheel before me.

Star and moon glitter in the turns

waves make storming

the Ōamaru beach.

I haven't gathered mahika kai

here yet. I don't like

swarms of kina, but

the ocean plants

feed me and my rainbow

and dried kelp carries the tītī too.

I'm fond of colours and kai.

They have things celestial

and oceanic in them. Who would

know my black foot

could create a star turn?

I sit within my colours,

my scraper inching along

biting rocks and seaweed.

If I had hands and a ukulele

I'd play 'Rainbow Connection'

for lovers and dreamers. La di da.

I look up past the salt ceiling

and ask how am I here?

A starfish plugs my breathing holes.

I push off a rock wishing for

fresh water. I have to feel

with my foot the sun.

Continuous Positive Airway Pressure Machine

When I breathe out of my nose the CPAP sounds like an oystercatcher
and when I breathe in it sounds like sea spray, rehutai.

On my cellphone app, SleepStyle, the bars tell me
how many times I'm disturbed in the night,

and how I'm breathing.
The bar-tailed godwit in the Canterbury Museum

doesn't make a sound. The laughing owl
is quiet. The museum took the models out

of the dioramas downstairs
that used to highlight our moa hunting.

I've popped my CPAP mask off
like a dummy in my sleep.

What if the taxidermist tried to wake
these birds instead of telling stories

about tangata whenua hunting
them to extinction?

Tōrea, kuaka, whēkau
sound better.

Pupurangi Shelley

I am a kauri snail kaitiaki
look on my green spiral shell
ye mighty and despair
I admit I've eaten
noke or native worm sushi
but I am *a hundred* millimetres
long and *move* at 0.013 m/s
through the Whirinaki,
the Tai Tokerau, Waitākere
and Kaimai ranges
to reside outside New World Gate Pā,
Pak'nSave Ruapekapeka,
and the Ōhaeawai Four Square
teaching our kids
their history at 2am or thereabouts
distributing udon noodles
from the dumpsters
so our kids can save the noke.
I miss most my kauri trees
with their big trunks
that sing with the wind
and admit they stretch
taller than my tall tentacles.
I tell the tamariki
our whānau whakapapa goes
for 200 million years
beyond the Treaty of Waitangi

and James Busby picked up
our tūpuna in a tentacular blink
twice giving us his surname,
Paryphanta busbyi busbyi
making it all about him.

Aroha mai, sorry,
I must eat and run.

The Paper Chase

I like to think that the original Treaty has been nibbled
by giant kauri snails in retribution for losing

their forests and everything they deem to be precious ☺
You can see their preambles along the margins of clauses

on the Treaty of Waitangi sheet, and the gobbled signatures.
They were trying to steal the deal, but didn't know

about the 1877 lithograph (darn it). They tried to chase
the other sheets too—the one at Manukau, the sheet at Kāwhia,

the one at Raukawa Moana (Cook Strait), the one at Te Moana
a Toi-te-huatahi (Bay of Plenty), the Tai Rāwhiti one,

and the Herald (Bunbury) sheet. Apart from the first and the last one
they couldn't keep up with all the treaties and barely

chewed on anything leaving the signatures shining as trails
in full moonlight and invisible by the light of day.

Maramataka

(Te Ono o Whitiānaunau | Te Whitu o
Hakihea | Te Waru o Rehua)

All the Phases:
Lunar Eclipse

Marama is a white kōauau
played in black gloves

She's a contact lens
or a very slow blink

She's getting long-deserved
shut-eye

but her tides
keep rolling

and the hills
are sliding into them

She's a takahē beak
or a curved door

up there closing
closing shut

but there is no red
moon here in Ōamaru

not yet as the space door
shuts the big tree in

Ehara i te rākaunui
Ehara ehara

A boulder rolls
slowly sealed

across the white hole
into sovereign blackness

Nearly there a curved line
shrinking

and then outside
it is faint red

Mutuwhenua: Te Awa e Rere Nei

((((((Medium Energy)))))))

For Dad

This evening we practised our waiata-ā-ringa with their composer,
Waiariki, at Puketeraki Marae. It was healing at Karitāne

to hear the beautiful words and learn the moves that speak
of our places of home, Hikaroroa, Pahatea, Ka Iwi a Weka. It's okay

to make mistakes and smile about them with others
who are your relations, and just to carry on carrying the airs

and graces of our whānau nui. Kāi Tahu, Kāti Māmoe, Waitaha,
Rapuwai, Kāti Huirapa. I've eaten shellfish and muttonbirds

in the weekend (at Hone Tuwhare's) and my fill of happiness
at Puketeraki. This kai is kōrero, from our whenua too.

Mutuwhenua: Mauri Ora Kāretu

((((((Medium Energy)))))))

For Mum

I need to feel the breeze of Tāwhirimātea
at Puketohunoa, to stand again behind Grandad's,

look across the valley at our Ngāti Manu marae
and breathe and breathe and breathe!

Ngā mihi nui ki te hau kāinga
who keep our whenua, our awa, te ao tūroa

as places to stand for ourselves,
and all who encounter us as ourselves.

I'm looking forward to coming home
in a couple of weeks. Tīhei mauri ora!

Whiro: 'I went alone to the Taj Mahal'

((Low Energy))

I went alone to the Taj Mahal
believing in love but the cabbie

asked why was I there?
And I couldn't answer him

as I believed in us
but did you? And my writing this

keeps closing doors
made of inlaid marble, nacre

impressed into memories
which I keep missing

for my mixing clay with marble
which never cures

for lack of an inferno
to turn the snows of our age

into cumulus silvers, pinks, blues
and golds over temple mountains

Whiro: 'The trees across State Highway 1'

((Low Energy))

The trees across State Highway 1
are young macrocarpas, I think.

Being a city slicker, what do I know?
Often, I see horses standing near them.

They're young too. Brown with heads
that bow into the field so they seldom

look at you. I saw them though
a couple of days ago at eye level

as my car pulled out from the driveway
and it set the scene for a lovely day.

Tirea: 'I was wondering why'

((Low Energy))

I was wondering why my energy was so low,
and I only had to look up past the clouds

the ones hiding our mauka
into the gradual background grey

stealing the day's horizon
making sparrows look vibrant

and any blossom pop
like a summer shirt

instead of days trucking
along asphalt

titiro atu ki te rangi
have a swim tonight

Hoata: 'Today's rain is like television static'

((((((Medium Energy))))))

Today's rain is like television static
so hard to believe that pine trees, swishing
traffic, young harakeke, chirruping
blackbird warnings, are real.

The water tank beyond the macrocarpas
is beautifully round, a rondeau?
While there's a pile of whenua
dug by the farmer next to it
with a yellow digger

that my boy would love to see
when he's here next except the digger
has gone for now. The radiata
hold out their hands like candle
holders in the rain—new cones.

Ōuenuku: Mauri Ora

((((((Medium Energy)))))))

Still raining. As an Aucklander that's nothing new
but for Ōamaruvians it is entirely, and we've had a wet

year. These wet ears have tried to settle
by buying a portable spa pool which bubbles

in the paddock, but now I'm worried to let
the sheep in because they might bite

my pool and so the grass grows longer.
A friend posted to FB this morning about ecosystem

benefits of birds and birdsong for mental health
and I'm hearing young birds, sparrows, chirping

at about the speed I'm typing this morning.
Speed doesn't make this Ngāti Manu younger.

Hmmm (I posted emojis on FB here). . .
Wish I could see Uenuku. Mana Pounamu is on tonight.

The awards are for our young people to give their hā
to the sky, who encourage us to thrive beyond

systemic concrete and neocolonial etceteras.
Whiti whiti, tata tata. Takoto te pai, takoto te pai.

Ōuenuku: Pukamata

((((((Medium Energy))))))

It was interesting to post emojis to my FB poem after I first
posted a draft as the emoji reactions switched to laughter

rather than the 'care' emojis that were there earlier.
Have I learnt how to manipulate Meta? Is this

the way into the matrix? I need to stop reading
about Keanu and get real. I have so many sets

of keys, including the lost ones from that poem
by Elizabeth Bishop, but I haven't found the lock

until just now with my newfound emoticons. Yuss!
I'm overthinking this. Looking forward to lunch.

Ōuenuku: Anei Anō he Rā

((((((Medium Energy))))))

I've folded Uenuku up into my pāua shell-studded
writing book and started whistling the Kermit the Frog song
again, *Why are there so many songs about rainbows?*

Sometimes I use my uncarved kōauau
which sounds just like my whistling
but I'm sure I'm blowing and not puckering.

It was a jazz waiata when I first brought out
my un-kōauau and reached out for hugs
made of Miles Davis brass. Now I know that to believe

in aroha, or love, is honourable and plain,
no similes for it except to say that love
has a purpose. Sure, I see things that remind me

of love, such as the gold over snow-capped mountains,
and the gold in fields of spring, and the gold
in dripping kōwhai blossoms that look sweet.

But they don't measure up really.
They're compensation. Those images are ideas
and lack the bite, kaha te katakata kicks and lick of life.

Okoro: 'I had a cat once'

(((((((Medium Energy)))))))

I had a cat once that liked to hide in boxes
so this is the place for that. There are unmarked

cardboard boxes, ones with 'perishable',
others saying 'Robert', some with torn lids

showing books, or old photo albums,
shoe boxes, and ones with cables.

Snowflake lives far away in Auckland.
I've been in Ōamaru for nearly three years.

I still have the dining chair with Snowflake's
scratches on it. We let her have one litter.

She was the happiest cat with her babies,
feeding them in a cardboard box under the stairs.

Tamatea Āio: 'And yes it is a peaceful morning'

((Low Energy))

And yes it is a peaceful morning,
fitting of its Māori name

except just like the problem
with my macrons being macaroon

typos, I've marooned one
on the word for peace,

unsure if my pre-coffee
inner spelling champion

has woken up as this wireless
keyboard has a broken backspace

and every time I start a line
Microsoft Word puts in a capital

which I faithfully delete as that key
is working still. Āio ki te rangi indeed.

Tamatea a Ngana: 'I saw a spider abseil'

((Low Energy))

I saw a spider abseil last night

outside the kitchen windowpane

after I woke at 4am. As the spider

descended a long white thread

it carried a white mass of silk

shaped like the near-half moon

sitting above the hedge.

Tamatea Kai-ariki: 'The pūrerehua walk under'

((Low Energy))

The pūrerehua walk under
the front door at night
and flap around while
I'm trying to write.

I bought a door sausage
and there's a curtain
but the pūrerehua love
the light and walk in.

One kisses the side
of my face (hemiface?)
reminding me of our kai
near Matairangi at Mabel's.

I forget the names of veggies
there, and elsewhere, but I'm
too hard on my meat eating.
Papaya salad takes time.

Tamatea Kai-ariki: After Talking to Jane

((Low Energy))

Thank you to Tāwhirimātea
who carries the birdsong and the seeds

Thank you to Ranginui who gives faces
to the sun, wind and rain

Thank you to the land
and the bloodied feet of marchers
from the scattered shards of hate

Thank you to the deep rivers,
ko te aroha ānō he wai, love's river,
e pupū ake ana, bubbling up
these rivers of tūpuna names

Thank you to the uku
of the rivers
making us makers

of whakairo
kōauau
of muddy fingers

Thank you for being here
to hear the waiata
to speak of tickled pūriri
to see a bird flop fly flop

Thank you to the whānau
and our dreams
remembering Rastas,
Nanny Mate, Nana Sarah
and Grandpa Paddy.

Arohanui and thanks.

Tamatea Tūhāhā: 'Last evening'

((Low Energy))

Last evening, I sat in the spa pool,

looked to clouds as the sky slowly

darkened, listening to Taylor Swift's

Midnights on the phone, so I kept

the bubbles off. After using the big

blue towel I noticed the clover leaves

had turned their faces down

in the dark. I looked at an email

about a furniture-moving bill.

Hung my togs on the line.

Had a shower to wash the chlorine

off. Drank blackberry juice. Then tea.

I couldn't settle. Wrote a poem.

Then this one. Planned several

more. I wanted answers. 'I'm the

problem, it's me', he sings along.

Ariroa: 'In your tūpuna whare'

((Low Energy))

In your tūpuna whare
I read and recited 'Karakia'
a poem about failures,
loneliness, angst and chance
sharing them around
as kōhatu in a sacred circle
giving hā to the four directions
to release them
singing a waiata
composed by our whanauka
about the mauka of home
Hikaroroa, Pahatea, Ka Iwi a Weka

The prayer wheel continues to turn
without its maker, just as the whare
continues to stand
with its flourishing fourth wall

Ka tū tonu ahau ki te whakamihi

Huna: 'I opened a box'

((Low Energy))

I opened a box and found my set
of Shakti Gawain cards. The author's
mother once sat next to me on a plane
travelling across the US. We talked
about writing and then she shared
how her daughter sold millions
of books. I later bought a copy
of her first one, and then
this set. The card I opened
this evening said that sometimes
it is better not to take the course
of action you decide on.
That it's better to be still.
I wish I had read that card earlier,
and many times. Them's the breaks.
Luckily, I'm visiting my mother tomorrow.

Mawharu: 'My basement got flooded'

((((((((((((((High Energy))))))))))))))))

My basement got flooded
and being a silly billy I'd stored
my books there. One of them
was *The Silences Between*
(Moeraki Conversations)
which was a book that kept
me going through my PhD.

I went looking yesterday
for poetry books
down an alley off Cuba Street
where I'd given a reading once
with Alan Brunton and others.
My poem was a repetition
of the word holocaust

Ho! Low cost! because Dame Tariana
had been dragged through
the media for saying it
about colonisation.
I found Keri Hulme's book
hanging from a peg between
Star Waka and *Catullus for Children*.

I bought them and the owner
gave me one for free.

Ōhua: 'Wet nosed'

((Low Energy))

Wet nosed, I tried to
gather summer's dew from a
paddle in winter.

Atua Whakahaehae: Alta Forte

((((((Medium Energy)))))))

After the very lovely awards
and poetic tautoko from Ruby and Arihia
and whānau tautoko
and Lauris Edmond Friends tautoko
and Verb Festival tautoko
with the party later
I woke up

Visited Simon at his Tuatua Cafe
and drank the most amazing coffee
thinking of his environmental values
like collecting mugs to reuse
from the tip to prevent disposable cups

Then I ended up gardening
at Anna and Simon's with Helen
and Angelina
I dug out the littlest weeds
going deep

Now marama has risen
Atua Whakahaehae
I can deal with this

The Para Matchitt bridge
gleams with pūrākau
light so clear and low
seagulls are lit from below

Atua Whakahaehae: Keening

(((((((Medium Energy)))))))

The kōauau made with uku
from yours
remains solid, played
but uncarved, undecorated
and it's unlikely
for my travelling
to be carved . . . yet
for me to learn its music
that is the next best step

Turu: 'Just last week'

((((((((((((((High Energy))))))))))))))

Just last week, at the memorial
for Keri Hulme with Ruby Solly, Arihia
Latham and Sinead Overbye (who brought
tears during her tribute to Keri), I also met
Gaylene Preston. We spoke about
Hone Tuwhare after the reading as
Gaylene had made a documentary about
him. I love his poetry and I loved
meeting him during his fellowship
at Auckland Uni in the early '90s.
I wanted to share that this morning
because I have an energy already today
I haven't had for years, and yes
I know it's a high-energy day on
the Maramataka. I feel like
taking a selfie with my blossoming
rhododendrons. I can and I can't
explain this very natural,
very normal quite unexpected
and quite expected meeting
just at the beginning
of no ordinary meeting at all.
I haven't had a shave but I'm going
to take photos and be brave
and share one on my main page.

Turu: My Funny Shoeshine Starling

((((((((((((((High Energy))))))))))))))))

Flaps, stands on a coned
radiata candle, sways
beak in feathered sheen

Rākaunui: Maranga Mai

((((((((((((((High Energy))))))))))))))))

The moon isn't

a multivitamin

she's the holder

of the tides, round

holder of the flooding

Taumārere and our

tarsealed whenua

'Kaua e mau riri

Anei anō he rā'

The sun will rise

and the mamae clear

the river rises here

when all the prayers

are exhausted there

But oh the mamae

until the sun shines

O moon draw me on

Rākaumatohi: 'Ka rongo au i ngā manu'

(((((((((((((High Energy)))))))))))))))

Ka rongo au i ngā manu o te ata
E hī ake ana i te atakura

Driving to Pak'nSave
after waiata practice
at Puketeraki
I drove by the beach
where to get pipi
my mind's flame
saw the pinkening
goldening
light resting
like strands of
glowing flax
on the waves
pīngao in the sight
as I drove
onward to Dunners
Ōtepoti where the poti
is woven into big builds
and not scraped
and beaten strands
no ocean spray
of rehutai just aircon
and Jess Cornelius
on Spotify
working through
difficult
stuff
in rock guitars
and song

Rākaumatohi: E Hoa

(((((((((((((((High Energy)))))))))))))))

How do I love you, my friends?
Let me count the mountain's ways,
the heightened plains that bend
up into snowy reaches, playing
on the mind out of sight to send
pillars of light, clouds, rain
on a grateful garden bed
pulling out rocks making lakes
with his tokotoko, with her cloaks sent
from our māra kai into our food basket
filled with sweetness and kōrero each
to each——we're peaches, plums,
strawberries and yams, we're
only the bumblebee's hums
aroha stumblefooting the air
in this flowering season.

Takirau: A Butter Lamp

((((((Medium Energy))))))

I know the dew today is fresh
from the birdsong, and if I walk
outside it will fill my nostrils...
it took a while to turn the lamps
off because who wants the moths
coming in again but when I open
the front door there's
the moon in Takirau
sitting a couple of hundred feet
above where the horses
and cows go for shade
with Kōpua above her
at her nor'east so that
I see the singing...
if I keep walking
and climbing
the taura takata
I'll reach her

Turi's socks
are on my desk
they're striped
with stars like this

Oike: 'Marama sits up in the west'

((((((Medium Energy))))))

Marama sits up in the west
looking through the dark
sunroom windows
as feather clouds
glide by on the sky river
hiding her in a crevice
until the horn of her
comes back as the cloud
pulls off her tree

And then she's back
and nearly round
arching and round
cloud glides over him
for a nine count

Then it's moon brightness
and then more feathering
sky as the light
slowly shows the tufts
of down edging

from the sun's rising tongue

Yet I fell hard
must get off the floor alone
change night into morning
all with my red hair turning grey

Korekore Tuatahi: Rom Coms

((Low Energy))

The night before the women's Rugby World Cup win
I watched two episodes of *The Crown*
where Imelda Staunton is the queen,
and the Charles and Di divorce
unravels from the Andrew Morton bio.
Now it's Renée Zellweger, Hugh
Grant and that chap from *Pride*
and Prejudice Colin Firth
in *Bridget Jones's Diary*
and the last scene
when she chases him
in the snow and he gives
her a new red diary
to begin again

On the soundtrack is Van Morrison's
'Someone Like You'.

I visited the Temple of Artemis once
and the Taj Mahal twice.
Off to Kāretu tomorrow.

Korekore Rawea: Karakia

((Low Energy))

When we close our eyes
in mihi to the divine
it makes us feel our tūpuna
our whenua
that we all
take a breath
in thanks
we shall not hate
that we will, love
reach out
and support one another
in shared
karakia

Korekore Whakapiri: Recycling

((Low Energy))

Hedges need clipping
grass needs cutting

but there is no Shem
Ham and Japheth

to trim them
and my power cord

for the hedge trimmer
won't stretch across

the paddock.
A feeble excuse.

I could buy one
at the hardware store

for instance. What's my
excuse then?

Better release the four-legged
grazers from the ark.

I'll let the magpies and starlings
sing 'When Doves Cry'.

Tangaroa-ā-mua: 'I slept under Puketohunoa Pā'

((((((Medium Energy))))))

I slept under Puketohunoa Pā at Uncle John's today.
Some of the valley is in lockdown. Kia kaha.

I can see the tōtara trees still
from the window sitting here on the bed

where Grandad used to sleep.
Everything is beautifully renovated

but the house is still the house.
Chickens used to run underneath.

The hot water used to come
from a kettle. Baths were in the creek.

We'd get mushrooms on the hill,
and run across to Aunty Bella's

past the outhouse. Her place used to be
the home of Grandpa Turi and Nanny Raiha.

It was that house and this house
that drew us in with their wairua.

Tangaroa-ā-roto: Star River

((((((((((((((High Energy)))))))))))))))

A uniform grey jersey
covers the day sky
but I know
that the star river
flows

Tangaroa Whakapau: 'I was getting a lift'

(((((((((((((High Energy)))))))))))))))))

I was getting a lift back to Whangārei
with Uncle John's friend, Judith
(ngā mihi nui!). I asked if we could visit
Uncle Jack and Aunty Margaret
first—luckily Margaret hadn't yet left
for work but Uncle Jack had already gone.
We drove across the new bridge
and parked outside the garage.
I'm just remembering the old bridge
which was a series of different-size
planks and railway sleepers
that rattled as you walked them.
We'd normally swim up this end
of the creek. I remember playing
with the bleating goats and their kids
with our cousins Scott and Joanne.
Aunty gave us a kiss
and we followed her inside.
I started crying (blimmin' tangiweto)
but luckily no one noticed
and I wiped my eyes
as I bent down
to take off my shoes.
I saw Uncle Johnston's tapestry
that he sent home for Nanny
Raiha and Grandpa Turi
from his service in Egypt.
He was killed in the Western Desert
in 1942 and is buried there

at El Alamein War Cemetery.
He had no children and so the tapestry
is one of our only reminders.
As we walked out the whare,
Aunty Margaret and Judy talked
about the camellia trees.
They're at least 130 years old.
Aunty Bella and Aunty Maraea
left strict instructions
to never prune them.

Tangaroa Whāriki Kiokio: 'Another grey day'

(((((((((((((((High Energy)))))))))))))))))

Another grey day, but when you think about
our colonial history, they're all Grey days
since his twice governorship and single
premiership bequeathed us a matrix
of suction cups (aroha mai, Keanu):
fencible cottages, block houses
and misrepresentation of pūrākau,
whakataukī including our sexualities
not only here but along every arm
of the islands described as wheke
by our tūpuna as if it was a wonderful
breathing communicating ocean
creature that stretched warm arms
over the equator and sucked
southern icebergs like going
to the fridge for a cold one
or was killing me softly
on the pinkest corals
fanned by colourful fins
but the English translation
messages us to die like sharks
and not to die like squid.
How do sharks die?
Why? Tell me why, tell me.

Tangaroa Whāriki Kiokio:
'I have never emptied'

((((((((((((((High Energy))))))))))))))))

I have never emptied
an eel trap, just eaten the tuna
which was fried on tin barrels
by Grandad and my uncles,
and it's raining today
so I need to resolve this energy,
and I've never hunted,
except for eating Roy's deer
he hunted near Waiouru,
which I enjoyed very much,
thanks Roy, but in general
just bought my meat
from butchers in Grey Lynn,
Ōamaru, Avondale, Mt Eden
and the supermarket chains,
and I've only seen crayfish
on ice and never in the sea,
although at the Waimārama marae
the tables groaned with crays,
which I loved eating,
except generally I'm living
an urban Māori narrative,
an internal migrant through
rohe that has translated me
still believing in the power
of whakapapa to ground
and feed me——Hī auē hī.

Tangaroa Whāriki Kiokio:
You'll Get an Email from Me

(((((((((((((High Energy)))))))))))))

The moon won't rise

in Auckland until after midnight

in Lone Star on Queen Street

after our English teachers' council

hui where we discussed

the future of English teaching

and how to include Māori writers

in the local curriculum for every school...

I've been grading here and writing here

in between, considering

how to make this work by reaching

out to friends for their ideas

about local Māori poets first,

and then local poets, and local Māori

writers and local writers

until we fill every school

in Aotearoa with our voices

because our voices

are recognised and loved

by our kids. Let's speak

at school like it's home.

Ōtāne: 'Virtue signalling in a time of Covid'

(((((((((((((High Energy)))))))))))))))

Virtue signalling in a time of Covid
popped in my head. I'm trying to remember
the words to our waiata about Karitāne
which I love. I'm yet to stumble
to the kitchen to choose between
dairy or almond milk, to switch
the ghost in the machine on
for my espresso, hī auē hī.
Twelve months and I'm tempted
to paraphrase 'All Too Well' (Sad
Version) by Taylor. I remember
the words now and I'm still
learning the actions.

Ōtāne: Second Coffee

((((((((((((((High Energy))))))))))))))))

For the second coffee I chose dairy;
blow it, you only live once (so I'm
using the only semicolon in the sequence).
The neighbours' sheep were in the paddock
last night which made me hopeful
I wouldn't have to rent a ride-on mower
but they've walked back to his place.
I was worried they'd nibble
the portable spa but all good
no worries at all eh. I'm going
to waiata practice soon.

Ōrongonui: 'Breezy vibes'

(((((((Medium Energy)))))))

Breezy vibes, says the podcast *Taringa*. I'm one of 'those
people' who says 'hauhū' instead of 'hauhunga'
in the karakia 'Whakataka te hau' 'cause
I didn't know better. Every version I found
says that, then I learn from *Taringa* it isn't a word at all.
Auē taukuri ē! And then I learn that 'aroha mai'
generally doesn't mean 'sorry', that it's clearer
to say 'nōku te hē'. Then the panel on *Taringa*
talked about intensifiers like 'rirerire',
'pohapoha' and 'mārika'. If you say
someone is 'ātaahua rirerire' it means
they are exceptionally beautiful. 'Mārika'
also has that effect to mean 'absolutely'.
'Pohapoha' does too, and also 'crammed'
like in the phrase 'ka kī pohapoha taku kete'
which means 'my basket is full to the brim'.
Tērā pea, ōrite ki te manawanui nē?
I hope I'm keeping my vibes breezy here.
I listened driving into Puketeraki.
It was afterwards driving home
that I found out about 'hauhū'.
Yesterday was an exceptionally beautiful day.
Inanahi, he rā ātaahua rirerire.

Ōrongonui: The Corrections

(((((((Self-doubts trigger warning)))))))

A little voice from when I was littler
telling me I can't speak te reo Māori
or speak at all, but I never heard.
It's gotta be coming from somewhere
but how did it get in here?
I can speak and I know that.

My voice kept me from doing
the work at law school. Voices
using acronyms trigger the inside voice.
Unsmiling faces trigger the inside voice.
Unenthusiastic voices trigger
the wanting-to-please-them voice.

Kia tōtika whakaharahara!
Get over yourself bro, get over it.
Tino waimarie koe. You're really lucky.
Mahia te mahi. Do the work
(and so much more).

Dunno why I'm dredging this up
'cause I did do the work. Ōrite
te KTK & te LOL!! Is it the ideological
state apparatus being expressed
in my funny bones? 'God knows
I want to break free', sang Freddy.

Roha ngā parirau o tōu manawa.
Beat your heart's wings.
Kia tau. Peace. (Sips Dilmah tea.)

Ōmutu: 'Some strange-looking insects'

(((((((((((((((High Energy)))))))))))))))))

Some strange-looking insects walked through the front door
last night (he ngārara iti nē). It's hard to keep them out.
I wanted to set one beetle in particular free outside
(I think it was one, hopefully not a borer bug)
but if I open the door then you know the score,
they'll all want to fly in. Even with the curtains closed
in the sunroom at night I can hear the thud
thud of winged-body euphoria on the windows.
Sure it's the lights on, could also be the rain.
Okay I'm in denial about the borer. There are little
piercings by the front door but it could be
the previous owner had a fine craft pen,
the sort with a little blade for a nib I'll use
to carve whakairo on my river-clay kōauau.

Mutuwhenua: The Whole World

((((((Medium Energy)))))))

Is the whole world going into Mutuwhenua?
I'm looking at *No Other Place to Stand* (te whenua,
te whenua engari kāore he tūrangawaewae)
and it gets me wondering about the end
of the whole blimmin' world. Blimey.
What will I do then? Can't swim in ash.
Can't plant akeake. Can't eat mushrooms
like our tūpuna, the ones that grew
on trees and were used for rongoā,
or practise as children on gourds
the tā moko tattoo patterns of our tūpuna
with plant juices from tutu and kākāriki
(pp. 98–100 of Murdoch Riley's *Māori Healing
and Herbal*). Soot from kauri was rubbed
into tattoos to make them black forever.

E hoa mā, please buy *No Other Place to Stand:
An Anthology of Climate Change Poetry
from Aotearoa New Zealand*
Edited by Jordan Hamel, Rebecca Hawkes, Erik Kennedy
and Essa Ranapiri (Auckland University Press, 2022)

Whiro: 'I drove home last night'

((Low Energy, so chillax))

...

I drove home last night after kai,
and yes it was kōrero, ngā kaikōrero
whakamuri, whakamua, and in between
in the present as the spiral
whakairo flexed and stretched
through whakapapa and mana
Māori.

...

Whiro: Waiata Whakaharatau

((Low Energy))

We learnt our bracket
of waiata ā-ringa and the actions
are getting really good.
I get a bit lost when the tāne
break off into the first verse
of 'Karitāne' while the wāhine
sing the second 'cause I follow
their actions but all good
I'll just wiri during that bit.
The main thing is to smile ☺
which is the best action.

Don't get me wrong,
I'm still going to learn them
properly. Mahia te mahi eh?

I got the Puketeraki T-shirt too!

Tirea: 'Ko Āraiteuru te waka'

((Low Energy, make time for loved ones))

Ko Āraiteuru te waka:
When the Āraiteuru waka capsized at Matakaea,
tūpuna explored inland during the pō, including
Ohikaroroa, but they needed to return before daylight.
When 'overtaken by the dawn' some ancestors
of Āraiteuru stood up as mauka, some were stilled
reaching to save tamariki, and this reminds us who we are.

Ko Hikaroroa te mauka:
Kā Huru Manu (kahurumanu.co.nz) says Ohikaroroa
was a tupuna on board the Āraiteuru waka.
The dual Pākehā name for the mauka, Mt Watkin, refers
to the missionary James Watkin who baptised the people
and hence the name was retained. Taylor (p. 107) says
Hikaroroa honours the Kāti Māmoe chief of that name.
In 1998 Ohikaroroa was restored as a dual name
under the Ngāi Tahu Claims Settlement Act.

Ko Waikouaiti te awa:
Where the awa meets the moana
is a beautiful estuary and mahika kai
cared for by the whānau.

Fascinated, I went back to the whakapapa charts.
66 generations to Ranginui and Papatūānuku
from Temuera, Eileen, Turi, Amber, Conlon, Trinity,
Shyra, Shade Nohotū, Chrystelle and Alisha
and 67 generations to Mu and Orin!

Hoata: 'Today at Ngāi Tahu Hui-ā-Iwi'

((((((Medium Energy, do something special))))))

Today at Ngāi Tahu Hui-ā-Iwi . . .

It was excellent to kōrero with Papa Bones
about Papa Kū as we sat on the bus taking us
to Arowhenua Marae. He wanted to be sure
that we placed a plaque naming the puna
at MIT's marae. Papa Kū gave the name
after a visit from children and partners
of people needing support at Odyssey House.
I also talked with Rino Tirikātene, who graciously
allowed me and Anna Jackson to use 'the tapestry
of understanding' proverb by Papa Kū as the guiding
whakatauākī for our close-reading project.
It was great to hear the whaikōrero,
and to hang out with Arihia, Ruby, Melissa,
Ariana Tikao and Ross Calman, and to learn the words
'groke', 'voyeuree', while buying an īnanga
fritter, perform the waiata ā-ringa with the whānau
of Puketeraki, talk to Eruera Tarena about plans
for 2050 for the iwi, and then to learn more
about taonga puoro from Ruby Solly.
It was there that Ariana gifted me
a wooden (I think it's made from rimu)
kōauau, and I also received a clay pūtangitangi
from carver Johnny Reihana. I spent
the next hours learning to play them,
and I'm still learning. In between,
I had a kōrero with my whanauka Katharina
who introduced me to Hēmi,
my colleague at Massey University,
who had read an article I wrote
a long time ago about digitising a whare

tūpuna so that it was like a virtual reality
cultural repository. I then played
in his digital whare from Awarua
wearing a VR headset! I also spoke
with Maha about the pounamu
he made that I was wearing
after many years sitting wrapped
in a koa wooden box from Hawai'i.
I only brought it out just today.

Ōuenuku: 'I tried playing my kōauau'

(((((((Medium Energy, a good time to connect with others,
    to learn and share karakia, or your pepeha)))))))

I tried playing my kōauau this morning
with limited success, just the hā coming out
although I got a reedy pitch a couple of times

but the new pūtangitangi wanted to play
despite my unpractised lips—
however I blew there was a note!

Oh it felt good to connect the breath
with this little moon—it really looks
like a small marama, except for the main

hole to blow in, and the finer holes
to help release the hā. With a bit of luck
from the sky we're going on a cave walk

later today. I drove home last night
like the Cyndi Lauper song in reverse
and could see the rain all through Waihao

came from Ōamaru. These gifts of kōauau,
mānuka honey and pūtangitangi
are tohu which don't need to be disclosed

and I accept them with a whole heart,
manawanui, from my whatumanawa,
my manawa, and my pūmanawa.

Mauri ora e hoa mā.

Ōuenuku: Hine Raukatauri

((((((((Medium Energy)))))))

I place the rimu
below my left eye
and the clay flute
onto my right eye
to help them
revive me
through tears
(inhale, exhale)

Kua pā ahau i te rimu
ki raro iho i tōku kamo mauī,
me te pūtangitangi
ki runga i tōku kamo matau—
mā ngā rerenga roimata
hei āwhina kia whakarauora rawa
(hā ki roto, hā ki waho)

Okoro: 'The star river'

((((((Medium Energy)))))))

The star river
is a deepest blue long ((open))-ing

in cloud banks mirroring the Waitaki
as you roll across the night bridge

       led by   .

    the horn   .

         of   .

       Okoro   .

Okoro: Honouring Words

((((((Medium Energy)))))))

For Kateri

Here in
this part of
our Waipounamu
((with
my tupuna
Maru))
I saw through
the night cloud
īnaka / īnanga / whitebait
but not the aurora
borealis I saw
in Ontario with you
in green curtains
dancing the horizon
ki tua o te ārai
(((beyond seeing)))
to the zenith
and firefly sparks
driving on
to Cape Croker,
Georgian Bay
where our tūpuna
continue the hui

Tamatea Āio: The Best Hours

((Low Energy, a time to be cautious—the unpredictable can
happen. Avoid hui at this time. Stay close to whānau.))

'I know those fault-lined hours best
so un-kōauau. The old push on the [*sic*] brass hug...'
I wrote at 18 with Miles Davis in the background.
Even with my three kōauau now that is how
I feel this morning. Cautious.
Unmusical. For the hui this morning
my mind clings like a pāua in the high tide
to the second and third articles (te tuarua
me te tuatoru) of te Tiriti o Waitangi. Self-talk:
Why always go there? Make it a kōrero about
manaaki, whānau, mātauranga, wairua,
tangata whenua, arohanui.

Tamatea Āio: Āio ki te Rangi / Rave On

((Low Energy))

My first poem was for my primary school teacher,

Mrs Naire. I went outside and wrote about clouds—

the alligator floating across the sky while I lay

in reeds watching it glide. As the sun vanishes

I'm looking at clouds again, more like paint splashes

with the last blue of sky behind them like other

paintings underneath a sky that recycles

its art. It has been a hard day today

and this softness is very welcome.

As the dark settles in for the night

the blue gains an intensity

like it did and still does in the Civic

with its thousand-and-one-nights

picture-palace set as the lights go down

and the film began and begins to roll on.

Tamatea a Ngana: 'Four kinds of akeake'

((Low Energy, still a time to be cautious.
Ko te Tuatoru: equal rights clause.))

Four kinds of akeake
yesterday to promise
rongoā with intention
to grow into the trees
our tūpuna used
to make hard
paddles and taiaha
hoea hoea rā

They sit in a cardboard
box like cats about
to find their toys and twine
among the harakeke,
kōwhai, mānuka
tī kōuka and tōtara
but these will be big
cats, five metres tall

for the front yard
and just under two metres
high for the fence line
with my neighbour
though I'll need a tube
or sacking for frosty days
for the red-leaved akeake
whose whiskery leaves

will twitch and stretch
in time so I'll start digging
with a spade, not a kō
though I'd love to.
Murdoch Riley says Kahukura
lives in the skin of Akerautangi.
Kahukura (a rainbow)
is a spy god (also the Facebook

atua) who reports on
Akerautangi's posts, stories
and newsfeed since Tū
uses Akerautangi to fight
Rongo, god of peace and
cultivated kai and so akeake
and Kahukura protect the garden
(self-talk: get some kūmara)

'Ka tukua ki a ratou nga tikanga katoa
rite tahi ki ana mea ki nga tangata
o Ingarani.' (macaroons missing
as per the original Tiriti)

Tamatea a Ngana: Kōauau—Te Wāhi Ngaro

((Low Energy))

After seeing a Richard Nunns documentary

Rātou mā...
The kuia came out when they heard
the tangi of kōauau and cried
saying they remembered them
from when they were young.
Tohunga still have the music
of mōteatea so the sounds
they make are faithful,
supportive, tika and pono.

Tātou ki a tātou...
Air floods in wells up
through our bodies
out of our mouths
and noses to flute notes
and sounds that step,
ripple, shimmer, vanish
((into)) ((under)) ((over))
((after)) ((before)) ((now))

Hear the hau ora
of our sheltering trees
their leaves speaking
by the life-giving breeze
Blow the wind into
this rimu here
and this clay there
and taste the air

Tamatea a Ngana: Two Questions

((Low Energy))

You would let me know,
if you love me?
You wouldn't
let it slide?

Tamatea Kai-ariki: 'Three birds flew from me'

((Low Energy, continue to be cautious.
Offer support to others.))

Three birds flew from me:

a sparrow from my chest
a tūī out my throat
a pīwaiwaka from my thigh

they flew to see my father
to let him know I am well

then the monarch butterflies
took their turns to see my
grandmother
once they saw the birds
were safely flown

and then the bees
came back to the field
to help the new mānuka,
akeake, harakeke, tōtara,
tī kōuka and kōwhai
bring back the birds

Tamatea Kai-ariki: He Iti Pounamu

((Low Energy))

Since you were a pēpi

I'd sing to you in Māori

and you'd hold

the pounamu round

my neck that I got

from Nanny Ina.

That's the first

thing you reach for

still when I lift you up

and we sing along.

Tamatea Tūhāhā: 'The last time we saw each other'

((Low Energy))

For Joy Harjo

The last time we saw each other
we drove up the ancient
stronghold of Maungakiekie
and I shared with you,
esteemed friend,
this was the centre.
You drew a deep breath
and looked out
across Tāmaki Makaurau
(Tāmaki beloved by many).

I tērā wā i kite nei tāua i a tāua
i taraiwa ake tāua ki te pā
tūwatawata o Maungakiekie, ā,
i whāki au ki a koe, e te māreikura,
ko tēnei te pokapū o nehe rā.
Kua whakangā koe, ā,
ka titiro roa atu
ki Tāmaki Makaurau.

Ariroa: When Great Trees Rise

((Low Energy))

After reading Maya Angelou's
  'When Great Trees Fall'

When great trees rise
they start small
taking on the dewdrops
in summer, bending
with the birds' wings
as they lift to twitter
in the blossoming plum tree
taking their time to grow
and grow and grow
up

Huna: My Own Personal Marama

((Low Energy))

'Marama. Ko Marama tērā',
I'd say and point up there. I told him

about Rona and the tī kōuka too.
Then I'd go and sit on the moon,

lifted by moths to sing from my
cabbage tree not unlike a little prince,

or David Bowie. I go up there and waiata
like it's 1999, cloaked in shuffling wings,

watching Papatūānuku from the sky—
change into a glittering pāua in space

to marvel at the sea, my whānau,
and being a piri pāua, at my home.

Mawharu: 'A respite from low-energy days'

((((((((((((((High Energy))))))))))))))))

A respite from low-energy days
(thank you Maramataka)
but I still can't see the sun.
He's far away with the celestial
whānau whose flag is never
upside down no matter how
you look at it. At least
with Māhutonga you
can sort of tell when
the Southern Cross
is oriented incorrectly.
E hika mā! When you're
on the USS *Enterprise*
the globe looks all the same
too. Round and round.
'Right round like a record,
baby, right round round round.'
So, even though I'm feeling
upside down, and downside
up, moi still looks the same.
Astronauts use straws
to drink from, so I think
I'll raise paper flags
on them, four to be precise,
one with each clause
of te Tiriti, and turn
them around a lot on
high-energy days like this,
ready for planting
on the moon.

Ōhua: A Short Short Fiction

((Low Energy))

After reading W. S. Merwin's translation
'Death and the Lover' from Flor Nueva de Romances Viejos

Last night among my dreams
about holding her in my arms
I dreamed she messaged me
on WhatsApp but it wasn't her,
it was Death who told me
God had sent him
so I begged him for a day——
he granted me one hour
to speak with my love.
I swallowed a glass of water
and splashed my face.
I sent texts, because it was urgent,
FB messages, and even left
a voice message,
'I'm on my way!'
I pulled on my jeans,
buttoned my shirt,
laced my running shoes
but none of these
reached her devices,
and no one answered
the door. She had
been stitching
a tīvaevae for us
and had fallen
asleep embroidering.
Then, I saw a heart emoji
on my cellphone
which I clung to
in a dream state
as Death asked me
to walk this way.

Atua Whakahaehae: Chains

((((((Medium Energy))))))

We travelled the motu,
strong tāne and wāhine toa
armed with mōteatea
to remember and avenge the fallen,
warrior poets. We brought our women
and men with the hardest backs,
with heart strength as the undying
house of the people.
We looked for friends and made
enemies who stopped us
making sense. This event chain
became a Queen's chain,
a mayor's chain, a speaker's mace,
fields of grass and daisies,
fox holes overseas, praise
for uncovered trenches
(e.g. Ruapekapeka, Ōhaeawai)
in the many revisions
that leaves Sir Edmund
standing on another people's
snowy mountain (and Tenzing
tested for speaking).

Turu: From My Sunroom

(((((((((((((High Energy)))))))))))))))))

The horse stood grazing
in the macrocarpa shade
then its partner walked away
and the first dark chestnut
horse followed nodding
its head as it moved
glossy flanks and shiny black
mane and tail

Then the cows galloped
across the same way
as a farm worker scatters feed
in the yellow and green field
swishing their tails

The mooing makes me
think of likes on my phone
as it chimes for each like
and to think the sound of om
between the truck sighs
gliding down and the truck
hums rolling up
and the many sweet sparrows
singing in the present day

Rākaunui: Shakti Card Opening

((((((((((((((High Energy))))))))))))))))

I will learn to enjoy this journey
into the unknown.

Two magpies sat on the power lines
this morning and I thought
they were pecking it
but they were just catching
their balance. They might
have been sitting on the manapau
tree in the underworld for all
I know, watching Māui
dropping berries
on his parents.

I drove the fourteen bridges
again to Ōtautahi, sending mihi
as I drove to Waihao, Arowhenua,
and each tupuna awa
thanking them for nurturing
the people. Stations
of the Cross? I'm agnostic.
It is a way of the spirit though.
A place where the whakapapa
flows like blood despite

rabbits nibbling
the flax. They've whittled
back the mānuka!
I imagined they couldn't
reach the top but they
must have bent it over—
one bending the young
mānuka down to tooth
height, the other
nibbling as a cooperative.

Putting protective wire up
is hard, and I'm outnumbered.
I need our gardening club!

Rākaunui: He Whenua Manu

((((((((((((((High Energy))))))))))))))))

Trigger warning: death, November 1769

On RNZ this evening
I heard a podcast about the kura,
or rimatara, a red-feathered lorikeet
from Tahiti and how it was almost
hunted to extinction
for its feathers by Polynesians.
It existed on only one island
in French Polynesia
until they moved 27
to Aitutaki in the Cooks.
It took many years
to approve this from
the French side
even though our whakapapa
speaks volumes.
James Cook brought red cloth
with him to Aotearoa
which our people loved
as we had not seen
the kura for centuries.
But even so, the trade
wasn't always a success.
In early November 1769
a man came aboard
the *Endeavour*
from a visiting canoe,
according to Beaglehole,
and reclaimed a woven cloak
he'd swapped
for a piece of cloth.

Then he left with paddles
'shaken defiantly'.
Lieutenant Gore
used a musket
to kill him. Cook wrote
that he thought it
'a little too severe'.

Rākaumatohi: 'The house shadow'

((((((((((((((High Energy)))))))))))))))

The house shadow is an eclipse over
the dawn's rising hedge. The camellia
is bisected, half-light, half-shadow
with a curvature which might be
a trick of the light as the Erewhon Road
continues ten feet in front of the hedge
also named the road to Dunners,
State Highway 1, my tarsealed
mid-shot with guts as close-ups
on a gullet lined with magpies
as flying orcas, splashed rabbit
possum furs and weka. Too urban
to stop and pluck the feathers
for weaving, too squeamish
to move the roadkill and protect
the kāhu. Oh, how vulnerable.
I'm not Irish enough for stew,
and I also came from there.
Wet wheels, blood. Shivers.

Takirau: Uku Rere

(((((((Medium Energy)))))))

1.
I give the clay
water from the tap
to save my drinking water
without the nitrates
to make this flute.
I cried a little
imagining this
might soften the clay
but no. Instead,
I made a fire—not
fast enough to
cup your hands
for my hands
to pour water
cooling yours.

2.
I made three kōauau
and learnt it isn't intuitive
to make flutes
from clay. I thought
I'd go natural
and use a stick
left by the previous
owner in a bucket
of water.
It's from a protea
and still sporting
healthy leaves

so it's going to thrive
once the roots sprout.
I poked the stick end
through the uku
but its shape
didn't please me.
I used a metal rod
to stipple the surface
but it looked weird
not like the kōauau
in my head.
I did this twice.
Rolled them back
together into a ball
after watching a YouTube
video from a teacher
and made the beginnings
of one kōauau.
This morning
it is still drying.
I haven't found
a video yet about
carving clay kōauau.
I intend to use
the pūhoro
pattern because
that's me. I hope
I find a good teacher.
Pai mārire.

3.
I roll the ball of uku
slapping it to get rid
of any air bubbles.
I'm following the video
despite not owning a kiln.
For a cutting tool
I use dental floss
dividing the ball
into two semi-spheres
which I cup
one at a time
into my left palm
using my right thumb
and forefinger
to pinch a bowl.
I join both bowls together
to form a hollow sphere.
I use a fine chisel
to form a blowhole
which I enlarge
with my little finger
and then hold
the hole in the V
of my thumb and forefinger
and mark a spot
against each knuckle
to make smaller
holes and one at the end
of my fingertip.
Now it is slowly drying
before I carve the skin.

Oike: 177 years

((((((((Medium Energy)))))))

Okay, yesterday's clay was dried by a hidden fire,
the return of Ōtuihu Pā which was destroyed
by HMS *North Star* and took Ngāti Manu
inland to Kāretu where we are now.
A version of this is in the journal
of Major Cyprian Bridge including
watercolours of the razing
of our Ōtuihu village. I went
to the beach with Turi instead
of sitting around moping.
This morning I saw some of the photos
of the celebration. The one that got me
was the wall full of photos
in our whare. I te tangitangi au.

Korekore Tuatahi: 'I bought the chart'

((Low Energy))

I bought the chart *Te Tau Toru Nui o Matariki*
and now know we're in the seventh month
Te Whitu o Hakihea (Menkent in Centaurus).
There is so much to know, lifetimes
of learning the science of our tūpuna,
but I do know beauty when I see it,
whether it is hidden or apparent.

Korekore Rawea: Q+A From a Shakti Card

((Low Energy, be creative))

Because korowai take
all the abilities
of their makers
they aren't made
on hunches,
and the īnanga
(kōkopu, baby tuna)
rippling in pounamu
are active and best
with huge love
but I wasn't ready
I lacked the insight
and went for a moon
launch when a go-cart
or a raft made
from recycled bottles
might have played
to my best abilities
plus I don't have
a roof rack for a kayak
which is what I'd love
to do, go kayaking,
or hitch my bike
on my bike rack
and ride round
the Waitaki lakes
rather than
moon shadows.

Oh, Shakti, I did
follow my hunch
but much better
to call beyond
the greenstone
on my chest
beyond this cloth
of knowing
that the veil
is going to lift
from the picnic
after all the games
of hide-and-seek,
the swings, seesaws
and slides
of birthdays
in the park.
Much better
to drink
the water.

Korekore Whakapiri: 'I threaded the eye'

((Low Energy))

I threaded the eye of Rākaihautū's
tokotoko as he wove our myriad
lakes. It was to stitch me back together
like an inverted poetry scarecrow
for birds going about their manu
and friends going about their human.
I have made these kōauau
from local clay, and gifted rimu,
with holes measured by my knuckles.
So my wings might be decorative
museum pieces, but it's the things
of flight, the getting past glass
cases conjuring shrouds
and stuffed throats. E rere,
taku manu. Kia piki te ora!
Fly my bird. May you be well!

Tangaroa-ā-mua: Ranginui

((((((Medium Energy)))))))

It's true we were pushed apart
by our son, Tāne-tokotoko-o-ngā-rangi
but he needed to breathe
and the myriad flying singers
needed to flap their wings
swirling and swooning
in their aerial chicka booms.
How could we make this
a sad thing in the telling?
Why make the rain
all about me and Papatūānuku
when there's all this growing
from the children?
There's a respite in today's
forecast rain. The leaves
tremble it off, murmurations
of pittosporum leaves
bending with every tickle
crooning a Diana Ross single
at the break of day. Tell me
why, but no need to hurry.

Tangaroa-ā-roto: 'I bought a book'

((((((((((((((High Energy))))))))))))))))

I bought a book by Brian Flintoff
at Jason's Books off High Street—
great little secondhand store.
It is a tribute to Hirini Melbourne
about taonga puoro.
I played the rimu kōauau
this morning. It is so good
to be home filled with memories
and ideas, plus even the keyboard
is working properly this morning.
All the keys! Mauri ora.

Tangaroa Whakapau: 'After checking my FB posts'
Or, never ask a genealogist where they're from

((((((((((((((High Energy, a goood time with creative
juices flowing))))))))))))))))

After checking my FB posts and eating
my Just Right brekkie cereal
and drinking my first espresso,
and after ordering the Ozzi Mozzie
zapper online, I came up with an answer
for the person who asked me
in the café yesterday
'Where are you from?'
and when I said, 'Ōamaru'
and they asked again
and I said 'I'm really an Aucklander'
and then they asked for my ethnic
background and I began to tell them
but they stopped me before I could
name all my hapū and European
forebears (only squeezed in the Irish),
I could have quoted the poem
by Keri Hulme about where my bones
are from and listed the tūpuna place names,
but I think I might answer, 'Papatūānuku
and Ranginui' the next time,
65 generations from them,
and my children are the 66th generation
from Rangi and Papa.
'Where are you from?'
I should have asked.

Tangaroa Whāriki Kiokio: Super

(((((((((((((((((((Surging Energy)))))))))))))))))))))

Mum is coming to stay tomorrow
so I've dusted, vacuumed, moved furniture,
got the place ship-shape. It's much
nicer here today, I must say!
Turi went on a horse ride
yesterday which was amazing
for him. It was a patient horse
who liked being spoken to
and patted before putting on
a saddle. Rosebank Running Bear
is her full name, Bear
for short. She hadn't worn
a saddle for years, so
she was extraordinarily
patient with us as
her kind owner Kerri
walked Turi sitting up
in the saddle, me at his side,
around the field as our friend
Elizabeth took photos.
Then Turi ran around too
a few minutes later
showing us his powers.

Tangaroa Whāriki Kiokio: Puddles

(((((((((((((((((((((Surging Energy)))))))))))))))))))))))

Puddles are forming and norming
in the driveway, and cars kick up
spray on the Erewhon Rd / SH 1.
There is no signage that names
Ōamaru in all of Canterbury,
and only one sign just out of Dunedin
heading north until you get past
Palmerston, and that one includes
Tīmaru (happy to be corrected,
DM me). But to be unnamed
is not to be unnoticed, to not
be singled out is not to
be unbeautiful, unarchitectural
but sumptuous in miniature
Ōamaruvian Pall Mall.
It isn't like Rome where the chapels
hide works by Leonardo, but
our chapel at Teschemakers
reminds me of Tuscany. I have
a spring in my Ōamaru step now.
Plus, as our tūpuna name
suggests, we are sheltered
mostly from the weather.

Tangaroa Whāriki Kiokio: Calling

(((((((((((((((((((((Surging Energy))))))))))))))))))))))

It was Tangaroa Whāriki Kiokio
when I heard the mana of your call
from the mahau
bringing a tear
you called me on trusting me
as a bird of Ngāti Manu
who has made a perch
looking to Hikaroroa
to my Dad's people
Kāti Huirapa / Kāti Māmoe
across the Waitaki
swollen with melt
from the snow blankets
of our tupuna Aoraki

te mana o te iwi e tū nei

so of course we had to pānui
in the whare
beneath the pōua's and tāua's smiles
lining the pātū
so we all could be ourselves again
sisters and brothers in poetry land
I read quietly because I was shy
but Tangaroa carries
us all beyond ourselves
into the air, into the canyons
and bellies of whales

112

the streaming midges
and sliding snails
of rock pools
and breath channelled
through uku
calling and calling
in the whare
of your hau kāinga

Mauri ora e hoa

Ōtāne: 'I need to plant the akeake'

(((((((((((((High Energy, a good time to ask for help if
needed, and to give back to Tāne Mahuta)))))))))))))))

For Prince

I need to plant the akeake
to remind me of our purple forests
as descendants and growers
of trees, while the soil is wet,
and the other tōtara. We put up
a wire cage around the replacement
kōwhai, but I ran out of others
apart from the ones
trapping the hinengaro
which are no use to trees
needing tree-shaped leisure wear
that is both claw and nibble proof
so tree-shaped Kevlar. But
that's dearer so more wire.
Yeah a sandcastle wouldn't
last around each tree and the bunnies
can dig. I stacked bricks
around the mid-size ones
but that's over the top and might be
too dark for photosynthesis.
A scarecrow with light-up eyes?
But that might scare the birds
and I love seeing them.
No I won't plant plastic trees.
I need to get outside and dig
to leave yellow, purple and green
dripping for the hive mind.

Ōtāne: Songcatcher

((((((((((((((High Energy))))))))))))))

I need a hopurangi to wear
these cares into soothing songs
so that the fernbird mātātā,
the tauhou wax-eye, riroriro
warbler, can return my song.

Ōtāne: Feeding the Birds of the World

(((((((((((((High Energy)))))))))))))))

The estuary in the Canterbury Museum sees an influx
of visitors from all over the world in spring.

Visitors from Alaska, Siberia, Mongolia, the Arctic Circle
who flew their way from there to here

which some call the antipodes and others call
Aotearoa and many call New Zealand

which are names for home. The locals here
think nothing of the annual migrations.

Your common hedge sparrow, your starling, your blackbird,
your tūī, your pīwaiwaka, your seagull, your kōkako,

your kiwi, or your ruru. They just get on with it
whatever that is! These birds in their glass cases

were warm-blooded once and they flew here
and they flew there—across the great sea of Kiwa

or up to that flax bush, or over to that tree
with flowers, or under that roof, or digging up

a juicy big worm for dinner, or a little worm
for a snack, or the occasional snail to crack open.

Ōrongonui: Petals

((Positive Vibes))

The petals have fallen through my hair
from reading you after a winter
not speaking. I'd buried
my finest woven sail.
Ah choo. And, hi.

Ōmutu: Rākaihautū

(((((((((((((((High Energy)))))))))))))))

thinks about driving to Waihao
to fetch some uku
to make a kōauau.
It's at Waihao Box
where you said the local boaties
couldn't stand walking
around your group of mana whenua
to collect uku for taonga puoro.
I want to play taonga puoro
like you.

It ain't easy. I still can't
click my fingers properly
let alone make a clay flute
in my head. It's the idea
that some boaties
are out there waiting
to troll me for holding up
their kayak adventure
when this billy-goat
wants a kōauau journey
for healing. Auē. I'm still
in my dressing gown.
If only Tangaroa
would be my valet.
Tomorrow it's
Mutuwhenua.
I don't even know
the tides.

Mutuwhenua: Light Therapy

((((((Medium Energy))))))

Blue sky and green trees
with passing cloud shade
moving at clothes-drying pace
as the stacked pine sleepers
light up in the sun's heat.
Roadside grass heads sashay
and ceaseless twittering today
from our sparrow denizens,
our native robin lookalikes,
our energetic starlings.
A good gardening day.
A good time to clear the gutters
and wear a sunhat.

Whiro: Poi Āwhiowhio Thought

((Low Energy, do chillax))

If I were a tuft of feathers
flying off a string, threaded
through a hue, I'd wonder too
about my purpose.
Am I a distraction
from the real entertainment?
What possible contribution
could I make to this
apart from my beauty?
I might ruin the sound.
Yet here I am.

Tirea: Mooring Day

((Low Energy))

After dreaming I find myself in the Mātauranga
Māori Collection amid the carvings
that tell the stories of the talking mountains
of Tāmaki Makaurau next to the desks
and computers where researchers
and people coming in from the rain
read and write. Whaea Merimeri
gave that place its name,
Te Tumu Herenga, the main
mooring place, a metaphor
for a chief. Most of the collection
came from Te Hukātai, which means
sea-foam, the name of one of the mauri
stones in the traditional house of learning
in the Māori Studies Department,
which is named Te Rehutai from memory,
the sea-spray mauri in light.
I can never walk away from libraries.

Hoata: Seek Kai Knowledge

(((((((Medium Energy)))))))

This afternoon I will
continue to improve
my knowledge of kai
thanks to Mum who
found the new potatoes
in the garden for roasting,
made the jelly trifle
and the stuffing
already. Meri Kirihimete.

Ōuenuku: Mā te Mahitahi o ngā Kairaranga

((((((Medium Energy))))))

1.   Ka pāngia ahau i te ongeonge nei.
2.   Hēoi, kua āhua pai au.
3.   Ko Papatūānuku kua tuku arohanunui rawa mai.
4.   Whakarongo ki ngā manu e karanga nei.
5.   E kimi kai ana rātou. E kimi kōrerorero ana hoki
6.   ki ō rātou hoa huruhuru:
7.   te tīoriori, te whakatūpato,
8.   te ketekete atu tētahi ki tētahi.
9.   E ōku hoa aroha, tēnā tātou katoa!

Ōuenuku: By the Working Together of Weavers

1.   I feel this loneliness.
2.   So, considering, I'm okay.
3.   Papatūānuku has given immense love.
4.   Listen to the calling birds here.
5.   Searching for food. Searching also
6.   for chats with their feathery friends:
7.   cackling, cautions, resounding
8.   calls to each other.
9.   Dear friends, greetings to us all!

Ōuenuku: Aoraki

(((((((Medium Energy)))))))

I walk among the shrouds
with throats of birds but I am not
Māui and tremble threading
the needle that looks like the kō
of Rākaihautū as he enters myriad lakes
despite the stuff between my ears.
I'm going to visit Aoraki tomorrow
for the first time, to visit our
rock-crested, snow-capped
tūpuna of Te Waka o Aoraki,
standing on the highest side
of the crashed spaceship of Aoraki,
wearing the children's pounamu.
I will tell them about the visit
to Aoraki with their Nana
and we will share this
among the whānau
as their proud mataora
tattoos arch and define
our sky world.

Okoro: 'Come closer to me'

(((((((Medium Energy)))))))

*For Aroarokaehe. After reading
some tūpuna entries in* Kā Huru Manu.

Come closer to me, said
Kirikirikatata, where the snow
endures, so I can see you forever.
Mauka Atua will be just fine.
So Aroarokaehe moved
to an even higher place,
Kā Tiritiri o Te Moana,
to be mountains with him
and others from the capsize.
But Mauka Atua was not fine.
Officials drew lines to him on a map
to fix their boundaries,
trying to chain the god mountain.
The government officials forgot
their own people's stories
when making these defining choices.
Forgot how to love the people
who had loved them as people too.
They needed to share their faces,
kanohi ki te kanohi.

Tamatea Āio: Redux

((Stay close to whānau))

I am indebted to Nic Low's Uprising *and* Kā Huru Manu *for ancestor
names, pūrākau and locations. All mistakes are mine.*

I walked up and looked at the glacier
lake under Aoraki. We had tried
to drive nearer to Aroarokaehe first,
in the other valley, where it's less steep,
but too many vehicles there.
Parts of ice shelf floated
in the green. That was the scenic
view, the one with whānau mauka
a clear cluster in blue and grey hues,
above the Haupapa glacier.
Aoraki was partly shaded,
covered their face with a cloud mask
that rose slightly over half an hour
as I leaned on a boulder
feeling like a helicopter parent.
Still, to be on *that* rock,
near the pōua, Kirikirikatata
with Aroarokaehe also visible.
Together with the mokopuna Aoraki,
and the braided rivers,
they weave earth and sky.

Tamatea a Ngana: Kia Tūpato

((Low Energy))

Bought three ebooks
this morning about the world:
Anthropocene or Capitalocene?,
Hyperobjects and *World at Risk*.
I need to do some reading
as I drive past Karitāne,
Waikouaiti, Ōtākou
imagining the forest
I'm going to plant here.
Mum flies back to Pōneke
this morning and I must say
my world is more orderly
(I have a proper cutlery
drawer and the garden
looks like one now)
than it was before she visited
and I seem to have found
my mojo for everything.
Tēnā koe e te māmā.
Favourite part was hearing Turi
calling to his nana to come
over to where he was—first time
he'd used Mum's name.
On my return I'm going to stop
in at Dunedin City Library
to read and read and read
more. Then to talk about forests
with a native forester who
we bought kānuka and mānuka
from yesterday and knows
how to restore the land.

Tamatea a Ngana: Huia

((Low Energy))

The Canterbury Museum caption card
says the huia *is* the only species of bird
to have a differently formed bill between sexes.
The female huia used her longer,
slender, more strongly curved
bill to probe into narrow tunnels,
while the male used his short, stout beak
to expose the prey. The tail feathers
were used by ariki and rangatira
as hair adornments. In Europe
after the Duke and Duchess of York
visited here and he wore one in his hat
this incited a craze for huia feathers.

'The extinct Huia, with the Saddleback
and Kōkako, was highly adapted to live...'
and I should finish the quote,
'...in dense forest.' End quote.

Tamatea Kai-ariki: Tautoko

((Low Energy))

After the visit to the library,
I searched for hours and hours
matching our whakapapa charts
with six volumes
of whakapapa by the person
who helped our Aunty Pat
thirty years ago to reconnect
us to the taonga tuku iho
(that's when Aunty posted me
her lovingly gathered Kāi Tahu
and Kāti Māmoe whakapapa),
fascinating as some
of the mātua tūpuna were given
roles and achievements,
so it helped the understanding,
and fascinating because
alternate whakapapa
was given too which showed
many more generations.
I went and watched
Avatar: The Way of Water in 3D
and yes, it is pretty good,
emotionally astute entertainment.
Despite the many borrowings,
though, it isn't indigenous.
There was more indigeneity
in *Thor: Ragnarok* directed
by our taonga Taika Waititi,
and in his episodes
of *The Mandalorian*.

Tamatea Kai-ariki: 'When Nana was in hospital'

((Low Energy))

When Nana was in hospital
for the last years of her life,
it was Aunty Pat, Uncles Des
and his brother Les who did
most of the visiting. I learnt,
as Nana had stopped speaking
English, that she could still
speak te reo Māori,
a language she never used
with the whānau. I remember
her astonishment that she
could understand my basic
level of Māori and I was
astonished she could respond.
It's a lasting memory
of her, wheelchair bound
but able to speak Māori.
I learnt much later
that one of our whānau
who was fluent
from our great-grandmother's
(Hēni Freeman) first family
would visit to kōrero
with Nana. I also learnt
of her karanga at the tangi
of her sister from our
first whānau. It's
a beautiful memory
to have spoken with
our tāua like that
with her heart and mind.
E kore e mimiti tēnei puna
o te whatumanawa.

Tamatea Tūhāhā: Keep Learning

((Low Energy))

What is strength?
The courage to lead
flocks across the sky
like feather cloaks
returning bodies
to waves of forest
and ocean?
Is that the shape
of a tā moko
whatumanawa?
To bring life
to cherish a life path
(Āraiteuru
is a star path)
before the baby
is seen?
Is this a meaning
for Ipukura?

Tamatea Tūhāhā: 'After writing this poem'

((Low Energy))

After writing this poem
I'm going to do some gardening.
Plant some kānuka
between the potatoes
and then get some
chicken wire with Turi
to stop the rabbits!

Ariroa: 'The Maramataka website today'

((Low Energy))

The Maramataka website today
does not tell me the energy level
for Ariroa, it shows
an eclipsed moon
but from memory
today is a good day because
the last poem during Ariroa,
Waihao was fresh and its uku
was still wet. Qiane Matata-Sipu
has a great article in *The Spinoff*
which says Ariroa has rising
energy and to rest. Another site
recommends giving back
to waterways today so I'll visit
Kākānui beach with a bag
and clear litter from there.
Better have a coffee
and play my kōauau
slowly. Then learn some
more from Matua Rereata
Makiha on *Waka Huia*
who learnt from our Karani
Mohi and our Karani Huru.
That's how our grandmother,
Nanny Matekino, learnt
from our karani in Ōmanaia.
Werohia ki Papatūānuku,
werohia ki tai, he tuhi māreikura.

Huna: Three Poems from This Morning

((Low Energy))

(i) He Tikanga Poipoi

We planted tī kōuka and a tōtara
in three different times and places—
one by a waterfall in Karekare,
one overlooking Ōamaru Harbour,
and the first tree under
Puketohunoa Pā (the tōtara).
Each tree is with us through
the dreams, the dark or lighter nights,
the kind or the blinding days
and the prayers we say and sing
and the songs we sang and prayed.
Manaakitanga lifts our children
high, so let me plant another
tōtara with two tī kōuka together.
These trees stand here tonight.

(ii) He Tamaiti Nohinohi

Sometimes he
gives me a flower
from the garden
and blows me kisses
as he walks
away up the path
to go home.
Last time it
was an orange lily
which sits on
my windowsill.

(iii)

I rangona e au te waiata
'Kāti e hine tō tangi' i te ata nei—
ā, nā Sheku Kanneh-Mason
tana whiranui i whakatangi.
Hēoi, āe, e te tāne nei
karawhiua te tangi whakaae.

I heard the waiata
'No Woman, No Cry' this morning—
and Sheku Kanneh-Mason's cello
playing. From there, yes,
let it out man, yes cry.

Mawharu: Ngā Rā

((((((((((((((High Energy))))))))))))))

As I mowed a third of the paddock
today—that's how I pace it—I could hear
Dad as I wondered if I should put oil
in the mower. The answer was yes,
look after your tools—he'd get me
to clean the car engine so
the mechanics would know
his is a car that is looked after.
When I came back to post
and write a poem, I saw on FB
amazing imagery of woven waka sails
and some taonga who I recognised:
Matua Bobby Newsome, and Whaea
Maureen Lander who I owe
great debts to. I remember
when I was Māori Studies librarian
at Waipapa and the visits
to Whaea Maureen's classes
where she'd get me to find
the library's copies of books
she had already owned,
I'd say a better collection
than the university library's
as she opened huge volumes
of pictures of weavings
from museums all over.
It's wonderful to see
these enormous creations
have travelled all the way
from London, revived
by Whaea and her rōpū
Te Rā Ringa Raupā
of māreikura and whatukura.
Wonderful.

Ōhua: Tāhae Jack, Te Tangata Nui and His Beanstalk

((Low Energy))

Somewhere under the moonbow, there was a boy, Tāhae Jack, whose whānau
had run out of milk because their cow wasn't making any, and they had
run out of Weet-Bix too. Tāhae Jack's mum asked him to take their cow to
the freezing works so that they could get money from the freezing works
boss. The boss was a wise accountant who reminded Tāhae Jack of a sparrow
as she turned her head quickly and balanced on her feet like one. She
gave him six magic beans. Tāhae Jack was so hungry he wasn't thinking.
He thanked her and brought them back home. His mother lost it and threw
the beans out the window. Some of the beans landed in the firewood,
others were gobbled up by the hungry mice, but one magic bean landed in
the perfect spot, right in the middle of a freshly dug rabbit hole in
the paddock. That night marama shone bright so that there was a moonbow
glistening under the stars. Two little bean leaves grew to twenty then to
two thousand that stretched up and up towards the heavens guided by the
moonbow and the stars in the southern cross to find a heavenly hook. As
the sun rose, the top leaves had crinkled their way to the ninth heaven
which is when Tāhae Jack got out of bed. Woah! I'm going to climb it!
It was higher than a mountain though. He put his hands out and asked
some of the birds to give him a lift. Twenty blackbirds spread themselves
along his arms and grabbed the shirt on his back and flapped and flapped,
lifting him at least to one mountain height. He thanked them as they
placed him back on the stalk. Then he climbed and climbed, past midday.
Finally, he got to a high spot made of a combination of ice and cloud,
like walking in the firmest crunchy ice rink. He saw a castle in the
distance and walked to it. Inside was a person cooking, a kind old woman
who smiled and offered him some rabbit stew. They both got a fright when
they heard large footsteps. Tēnei au, tēnei au, a large voice cried.
The kind woman told Tāhae Jack to hide in the cupboard. He tangata nui ia!
He was a giant! The tangata nui ate a large bowl of stew, saying he
could smell the blood of a boy. Tāhae Jack held his breath. The giant
called for his kiwi. Imagine Tāhae's astonishment when it hatched eggs
made of pounamu, and he was just as astonished when the giant's pet weka
hatched eggs of gold. Well, you know the rest of the story from here
whānau. Mauri ora.

Atua Whakahaehae: The Humours

(((((((Medium Energy)))))))

Earth, air, fire and water. Put one of these
elements in a poem to make it exist
in the world, a microcosm
of the humours which is medicine
credited to the Greeks
but is itself an imbalance
of history better acknowledged
for Egyptian and African science.
This morning my body
is in balance after having
eaten a chocolate mousse
and cheesecake last evening,
but having justifiably visited
the gym first. I really
enjoyed it! Like this body
is for once a cathedral
with singing.

Atua Whakahaehae: Inanahi

((((((Medium Energy)))))))

Atua whakahaehae rise and play
with gods of the supermarket,
gods of airpoints and paywaves,
gods who deal out gout,
eczema and love,
gods bred to breed gods
as they shout and play

E Tū
Te Rā!
Hine!
Te!
Io!
Hine!
Io!
Te!
Tū!
Rā!

And repeat (kōrero anō)
like a game of tītītōrea
throwing kupu like sticks
as we clap and chant

Turu: Calm and Beauty Out There

((((((((There's a place for us)))))))

The end of the lunar cycle
so a calm without the need
for our gods to assert
or whakatika the many
balances required
for a world of light
to exist within the blackness
of never-ending space
where a thought
makes a quantum
adjusting connection
with a graviton
a photon and black matter
within a bubble
travelling faster
than light within
the dreams of our techiest
tech techies
who watch for
the next indigenous *Star Wars*
from Taika
knowing this is a paradox
to depend on an ideological
space apparatus
to save us from
a super-diverse
hyper-industrial
solar-system-wide
military complex
with a little dream bubble
in a god's shaken martini

Turu: Hoki Whenua Mai

(((((((((((((((High Energy)))))))))))))))))

Matariki will rise again over Ōtuihu
and like our tūpuna we will stand there
to repair the scarred fortress here,
inside ourselves. So shine bright
Matariki and bring us your healing light
beyond masts, canvas sails and booms
remembering our homes exploding before
their passing North Star.

We know the kōauau best...
the ponga, the kererū,
the pāua, the tōtara and mānuka-
scented kai, how to roast poaka,
smoke tuna, kiss kina and kōura,
find kūmarahou planted
inside our pā, eat kanae

for the ahi kōmau
is our enduring fire
within hand-adzed trees filled
with smouldering grasses
mosses and leaves
lightly scattered in ash
                        for future
fires to seed more waka, make
kai and keep the whānau warm
knowing Matariki will lift
our sap to the full moon
Ō! recalling sunshine
for our tender shoots

141

Acknowledgements

In some of these poems I refer to people by first name only. Waiariki Parata-Taiapa is a composer of waiata and mōteatea who leads our Puketeraki kapa haka / waiata group with great purpose and a strong mission. Arihia Latham, Ruby Solly, Ariana Tikao and Ross Calman are all noted authors in their own right. E kā whanauka, e kore e mimiti kā mihi ki a koutou katoa.

Many friends on Facebook offered support with their comments, emojis and likes as poems were posted there. Tīhei mauri ora! As always, friends and family have directly contributed to these poems. I am grateful! I'd especially like to thank Rauhina Scott-Fyfe for her advice on te reo Māori usage in the poems, and thanks again, to Ross. All of the hapa in my poems are my own!

Thanks to Word Christchurch for giving me the opportunity to write and read the poems set in the Canterbury Museum. Thanks to Mary McCallum and The Cuba Press for publishing 'Pāua Canticle' in *More Favourable Waters: Aotearoa Poets Respond to Dante's Purgatory* (The Cuba Press, 2021), and to essa may ranapiri and Michelle Rahurahu for re-publishing it in the first issue of *Kupu Toi Takataapui*. Thanks to Chris Tse, Jeremy Hansen and Auckland Writers Festival for displaying 'E Hoa' in the Britomart Precinct. Thanks to Charmaine Papertalk Green and John Kinsella for publishing 'Pupurangi Shelley' in their forthcoming animal rights anthology. Many thanks to Lynley Edmeades for publishing several of my poems in *Landfall*.

In the poem 'Maranga Mai', two lines in te reo Māori come from the Ngāpuhi waiata of that name. In the poem 'Ko Āraiteuru te waka', the reference to Taylor comes from the Kāi Tahu online atlas *Ka Huru Manu*. The lyrics in 'A respite from low-energy days' are from the Dead or Alive song 'You Spin Me Round'. Nic Low's *Uprising: Walking the Southern Alps of New Zealand*, Murdoch Riley's *Māori Healing and Herbal* and Queen's song 'I Want to Break Free' are cited in some poems as well.

My gratitude once again to Sam Elworthy, Sophia Broom, Kiri Piahana-Wong, Anne Kennedy and all of the excellent team at AUP for supporting my work since 1990.

Robert Sullivan (Ngāpuhi, Kāi Tahu) is the author of nine books of poetry as well as a graphic novel and an award-winning book of Māori legends for children. He co-edited, with Albert Wendt and Reina Whaitiri, the anthologies of Polynesian poetry in English, *Whetu Moana* (2002) and *Mauri Ola* (2010), and an anthology of Māori poetry with Reina Whaitiri, *Puna Wai Kōrero* (2014), all published by Auckland University Press. Among many awards, he received the 2022 Lauris Edmond Memorial Award for a distinguished contribution to New Zealand poetry. He is associate professor of creative writing at Massey University and has taught previously at Manukau Institute of Technology and the University of Hawai'i at Mānoa. His most recent collection was *Tūnui | Comet* (Auckland University Press, 2022).